THE POET IN ME

SHRUTI LAD

Copyright © Shruti Lad
All Rights Reserved.

ISBN 978-1-63806-146-5

This book has been published with all efforts taken to make the material error-free after the consent of the author. However, the author and the publisher do not assume and hereby disclaim any liability to any party for any loss, damage, or disruption caused by errors or omissions, whether such errors or omissions result from negligence, accident, or any other cause.

While every effort has been made to avoid any mistake or omission, this publication is being sold on the condition and understanding that neither the author nor the publishers or printers would be liable in any manner to any person by reason of any mistake or omission in this publication or for any action taken or omitted to be taken or advice rendered or accepted on the basis of this work. For any defect in printing or binding the publishers will be liable only to replace the defective copy by another copy of this work then available.

I am dedicating this book

To my

Loving Parents

Mr. Mukeshkumar Lad

And

Mrs. Trupti Lad

Contents

Preface *vii*

1. Pen's Dream — 1
2. Online Classes — 3
3. Sky Is Beyond — 5
4. Paper — 7
5. Mind — 9
6. Google — 11
7. Feelings With Bestiee — 13
8. I Want To.. — 15
9. Trees — 17
10. Dreams — 19
11. I Like To.. — 21
12. Clouds — 23
13. Seek For Satisfaction — 25
14. Poet In Me — 27
15. Google Forms — 29
16. Kites — 31
17. Mother — 33
18. The Masked Face — 35
19. Teachers — 37
20. Smile — 39
21. Life — 41
22. Good Bye 2020 — 43

Preface

In response to my small hobby of writing and based on my imaginative skill gifted by the almighty God and after the great support of the readers, I have decided to get published my second book of poems named "The Poet In Me". I would like to thank my parents, teachers, all the relatives and friends who have always encouraged me to continue writing. Most importantly, my uncle, Shri Avinash Parikh, a Gujarati writer and the winner of the "Sahitya Academy Puraskar", helped me at various stages by getting published many of my poems in newspapers, which was like a booster for the poet in me. Dear readers, please share your opinions about this venture of mine. Also, do check out my first book "Dancing Words" if you have not read it yet. Thanks For Choosing My Book.

-Shruti Lad
Mob:- 9173980627
E-mail:- shrutilad242@gmail.com

1. Pen's Dream

*My pen is eager
To have something written.*

*But mind is in trouble,
To get some words,
That would burst,
Fulfil the thirst,*

THE POET IN ME

Removing the dust,
Make such an impact,
Mind would be force to visualize.

And then would realize,
After a long span,
When they become old man,
Even though forget words,
But they have an idea,
Hanged in mind.

It would give them feeling kind,
And will find for same words.

My pen is eager,
To fulfil it's dream
And fill face with grin.

2. Online Classes

The trend of online become vast
Lectures at school become online class.
Black Board has got cleaned,
The hugs and hifi with friends.,
Got namaste that too on mobile screen.
The big airy class room,
Got locked on 5-6 inch mobile screen.
The mischief of classroom
Are overtaken by internet issues.
The period bells converted
To notification of meeting links.
The fish market noises from students,

THE POET IN ME

Got burried by mute button.
The charm of class got lost,
With angry shouts of teacher locked.
Actual meet became virtual
The end of lecture become punctual.
Notes changed to pdf file,
Made lively class online.

3. Sky Is Beyond

My face was filled with grin,
Seeing the work I did.
Seeing smile of family,
I got happy.
But it was temporary,
When I saw surrounding,
There were many roaming
Who were far better than me.

THE POET IN ME

My mind started to ask
Am I even fraction of that part?
My confidence got hinder,
The appreciation felt little bitter.

But then I remember
It's never over.
Let the efforts go on,
As the sky is beyond.

To reach the top,
First I need to pop,
The laziness in my thought.

4. Paper

Life of paper
Is lighter than air,
Heavier than rock
Depending on containt it owns.
Some are kicked off
From home by making a pile
While some are stored in file.
Some fly in air as plane,
Some float as boat

THE POET IN ME

While some have secrets of both.
Some have privilidge
To have a golden frame,
While some are put
In dustbin yard by crane.
Let the e-media may succeed
But the fragrance of page
Can never be achieved,
Some are light,
They carry smiles,
By giving big relief.
While some can make it heavy,
By tears it carry.
Life of paper
Is lighter than air,
Heavier than rock
Depending on containt it owns.

5. Mind

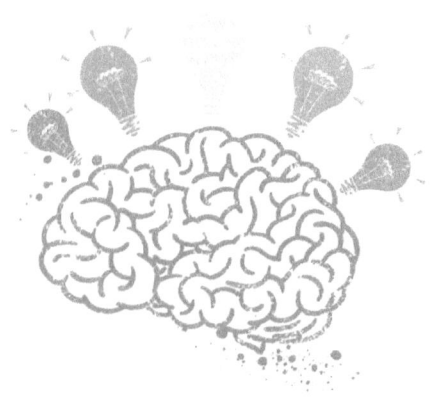

A small store
Which has many things to store
We feel it is full
It tries to make us fool.
It functions day and night
Helps us for everything to find.
It is the friend
Present to take any step.
Happy sad many moments it has
Just like air,

THE POET IN ME

Present everywhere.
At time of study,
It thinks to party
And at party,
It gambles now what will happen of study?
Useful-Useless many things
Are allowed to enter,
But closes its gates
When Q/A wants to enter.
It's like a naughty kid
Difficult to tackle.
Mind with a short circuit
Can make any invention,
That may result,
To floods of disturbance
Or curb problems on earth.
And can even take out of world.

6. Google

There is a friend
Whose memory has no end.
You will get tired of asking questions,
He's there with ready answer.
He is always free,
To give answer in brief.
He came flying,
And dictionary escaped running.
That friend is, Goggle Search Engine.

THE POET IN ME

Google seems good,
But our minds got ruled.
Brains became lazy,
To think question tricky,
As we have Google Baba sitting.
Now it seems little bad,
As mind become hazy,
We become it's dependant,
And we again ask google
For it's solution.

7. Feelings With Bestiee

Oh my Beastie,
Something has went fishy.
The talks which never ended,
Now needed topic to get started.
The work load I guess,
Became our obstacle.
This silence now
Needs to be tackled.

THE POET IN ME

It was just when thought pop,
Here the phone rung.
Silence cracked, Smiles hanged,
Time melted but
Talks not ended.
But after that,
Again the silence spread,
Seeing the message you sent.
A part of me was happy
For success you will be having,
But your news of departure,
Made me depressed.
But I was contented,
As clouds separate,
But remains in sky itself.
The eternal love never gets distorted.

8. I want to..

I want to sing,
I want to dance,
I want to study,
I want to play,
I want to do something great.
Hours and Days passes,
But I am stuck in the same
I want to...

THE POET IN ME

Eyes are needed to be closed,
To dream something big,
But also to be opened,
For making it happening.
The ladder to be climbed
Is big I know,
Then too I was stuck in
I want too..
One fine day,
I decided to take a step,
Some came to break,
And many to support.
Then I realized,
It's better late,
Than never...

9. Trees

Grown in dark
Surrounded by soil,
Pampered with
Water and sunshine.

A tiny leaf popped out

THE POET IN ME

To see the world around.
Days after days passed
Other leaves joined them all.

It started growing tall and strong,
Dancing with wind
And shining with sunshine,
Turned into a big tree.

I spread my arms
Loaded with leaves
To give cool breeze.
But my arms got cut,
I got hurt.

The branches that gave shade,
Became a problem for them.
But I keep my arms spreading,
For the happy birds that are chirping,
For face that smile by my shade,
I will keep growing for them.

10. Dreams

Small or Big,
Cute or Dreadful,
Gives pleasure or horror,
It does not follow anyone's order.

It's approach never assure,
Uncertainty even in happening true.
I am talking about dreams

THE POET IN ME

*Which can give screams
Or even pleasant sleep.*

*As the eyes open,
Often activates skip button,
Forgetting what had happen.
But often sticks in mind
And force to think,
Was there any hidden hint?
To be taken care
Before doing any deed.*

*Dreams often build a ladder
As it want us to reach higher.
Whether in day or night,
No matter what time,
What matters is action and passion,
For making dream reality with perfection.*

11. I Like to..

I like to see sun,
Of orange-red colour.
Which is rising,
With many birds flying.
I like to feel,
That cold breeze,
That can make anyone freeze.
I like to hear,
The chirping birds,
Their melodious tune,
Is such a dear.

THE POET IN ME

But I always feel,
Just for a day,
Can't they take rest,
And sit in their nest.
As best of all,
I like the sky,
Full of kites.
I like to see
Battles of kite,
I like to hear
The loud music in air.
I like to run
Behind kite that is cut,
And I like to scream
When other's kite get cut.
Happy Uttarayan....

12. Clouds

Staring at the sky,
Those birds that fly,
Unbounded blue sky
With the white clouds that float,
Like a boat in water.
Clouds keep sliding
As the wind shows path.
Don't have a steady stay,
Making new friends on its way
Makes various shapes,
But that too not steady.
Clouds are always ready

THE POET IN ME

To observe new things,
As they know
Nothing is steady.
It's better to flow with time.

13. Seek for Satisfaction

Everyone is sick,
To seek advice,
To be rich.
They want it just
At a blink of eyes,
And reach destination
That's the goal of life.
They want it's path
To be nice,
But tell them it is

THE POET IN ME

Of both fire and ice.
Few of them reaches the height,
Their seek for pleasure
Guides for proper action,
To dive in pool of satisfaction.

14. Poet In Me

Whenever I am disturbed,
Or any great is going to happen,
Whenever I see something new,
Or something old that's new for me,
My brain starts humming like a bee.
Few lines comes and goes,
Over my brain,
Thoughts run like train.
I want to talk to someone,
And when no one ready to hear,

THE POET IN ME

Pen and paper comes flying,
Telling me, "We are there."
I think to write,
Thoughts suddenly overload,
Or mind goes on strike.
I give pen race like a bike,
And here awakes the poet in me.
With the poetry ready on page.

15. Google Forms

Google has no full stop,
Always having someting
Or other to pop,
Like it introduced the google forms.
Which were meant for survey,
To give new products a way.
Used as an appliction form,

THE POET IN ME

To apply various events.
Eventually also became a question paper,
Which students have to answer.
Google forms got varied forms,
And we started receiving
A new link, every next day.

16. Kites

Kites are best example,
To give life's sample.
Any gust of wind,
Can help us to win,
And reach the sky.
But to reach high,
We need a good stratergy.
Flying free is good,
But sometimes we need
To duck ourselves down.

THE POET IN ME

We need to play wise,
To keep ourselves survive.
Battles are unavoidable,
We have to undergo cuts,
It can be ours or even of others.
But like kites we neeed to keep,
Our roots to ground.
Once it unroots,
There are chances to get wound.
Like those kites hanging
At the various poles and trees.

17. Mother

I have a mother
Always doing somethinng or other.
No one can predict her mood,
Is she happy or rude?
Pitty me went to her,
Asking Mumma,
Are you busy in some work?

THE POET IN ME

The answer flied,
Have you done your Home work?
Seeing the sign of danger,
I ran to other room in fear.
Next moment she was there,
Asking wheter I had snacks,
Predicting her unpredicted nature,
I ran to her,
To have snacks together.

18. The Masked Face

The variety of masks
A face can grasp.
A Mask of friendship,
Making enemy mislead.
A mask of anger
Covering deep love.
These masks when ajar,
Shows various emotion,
Some to hide action,
Some for making perfection.

THE POET IN ME

As many emotion grow,
It is persistant of masks shown.
It continues since when
That we can't ditch it
Then becomes part of face.
In this masked world
Now there is one more mask
Which has the task
Of keeping healthy
And give safety.

19. Teachers

Parents teach us to talk,
to walk, brush, bath....
But manners, knowledge, method to write,
In a way, everyone likes,
Is taught by teacher in school.
God understood our thurst for knowledge,
And our need to be led.
So he created a person,
Who can teach lessons,
And go in brain of students,

THE POET IN ME

Whom we call teacher.
Teachers are dedicated, to education.
This is their passion and our liberation.
They do not just make us study,
Also encourage to achieve our goals.

20. Smile

Just spreading of Lips,
Can make one's heart heal.
After a long day,
When brain gets locked,
Just a cute innocent smile,
Can be a master key.
It's best ornament of face.
Worried about something,
Or trying something new,
And seeing a smile,

Boosts inner confidence,
Satisfaction for our action.
Smile is an art,
To mend sad heart.
Smile is not a thing,
To be stored in file,
It is infection of happiness,
To be spreaded everywhere.

21. Life

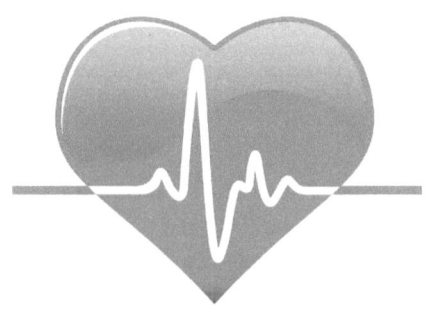

What is use of life,
If you just want to criticize!
Many things are there,
That have to be achieved.
Many spots are there
That are left to be visited.
Life is a game
Of Snake and Ladder,
Many snakes are spreaded
To pull down our leg,
But also ladders
To pull us up.

THE POET IN ME

Ups and Downs are spikes,
That are part of game,
If I am not wrong,
Heart beat also have same shape.
Any numbers can occur,
But we can always conquer.
As what is the use of life,
If you just want to criticize!

22. Good Bye 2020

January started with smiles,
Everyone flying like kites.
February, March were busy
In welcoming Trump.
All these months had fun.
Then a virus started shooting
Everyone with gun.
Lockdown was immediately done.

Everyone's temper started to burn,
The story don't need replay,
Let's all pray, New year

THE POET IN ME

Starts and Ends with smiles,
Happiness loaded on all it's files.
With a big GOOD BYE 2020.

www.ingramcontent.com/pod-product-compliance
Lightning Source LLC
LaVergne TN
LVHW041549060526
838200LV00037B/1207